HOW DO OUR *Feelings* CHANGE?

AUTHORS: LOLA LAWSON AND LIVITY LAWSON-BERNARD

ARTWORK CREATED BY: LIVITY AND MENELIK MAKAI LAWSON-BERNARD

To order additional copies of this book, contact:
Xlibris
844-714-8691
www.Xlibris.com
Orders@Xlibris.com

ISBN: Softcover   978-1-5035-7317-8
         EBook   978-1-5035-7316-1

Print information available on the last page

Rev. date: 02/02/2024

How Do Our Feelings Change?

Words of gratitude

We are truly grateful to our relatives and friends for their love and support.

Very special thanks to Yukina Hamamoto, Motoka Murofushi and Sujon Sugi for your extraordinary generosity, and grateful thanks to Susan Macpherson and Deb Stanbury for all of your kindness.

~Lola

Dear Reader,

In your hands is a time stamp of the life of my children, in the very early stages of their development. I honour their presence and every part of their essence by infusing my love for them into this book.

What you are holding is a very small part of the everlasting and deeply compassionate caring that I have towards my children.

Thank you for becoming an integral element of a vision that has come into existence through love.

When I feel sad, what can I do?

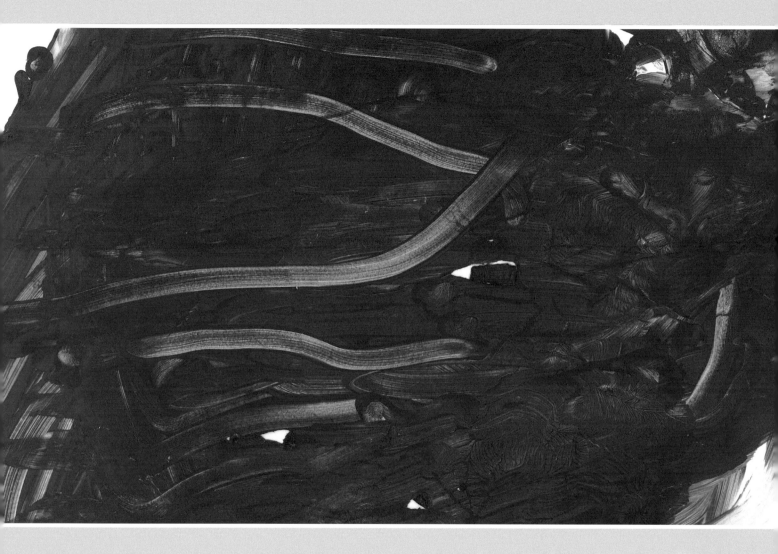

I can take a deep breath
to remind me of the way
my body moves.

When I feel lonely, what
can I do?

I can care for others,
which helps me to feel
better too!

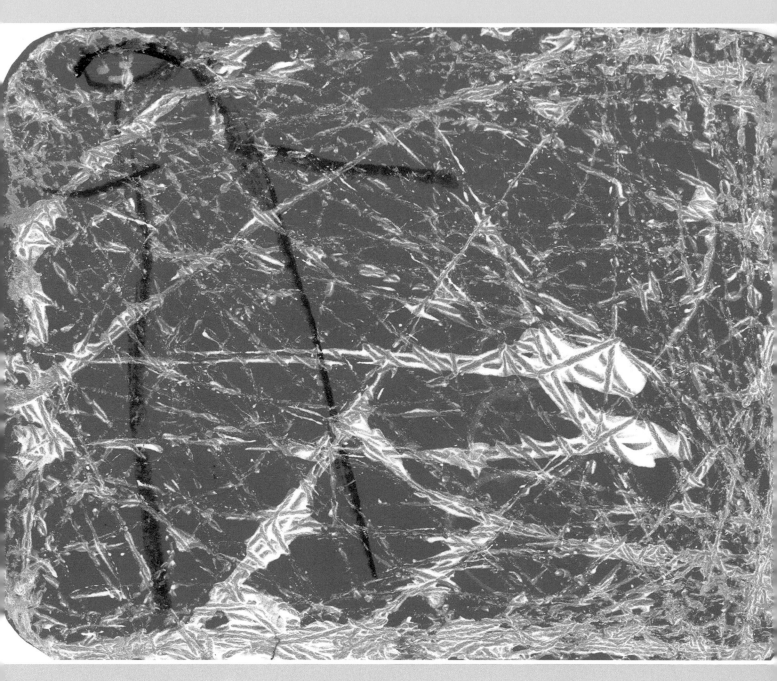

When I feel grumpy,
what can I do?

I can dance to a happy tune.

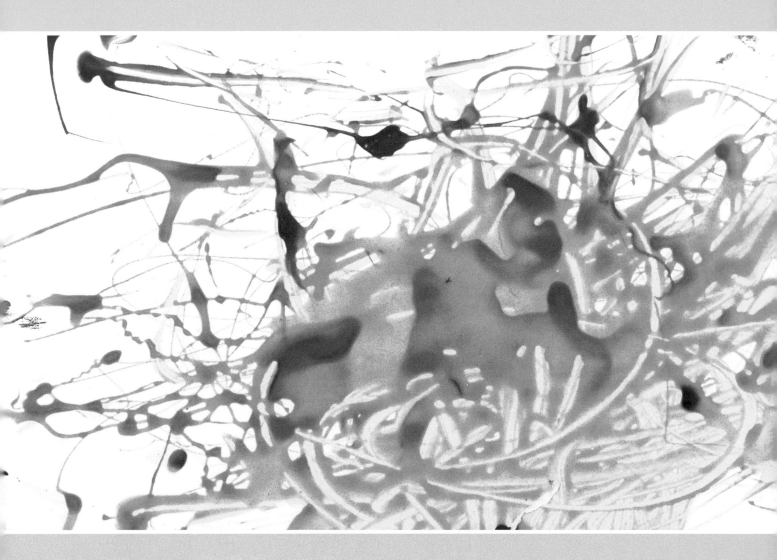

When I feel shy, what
can I do?

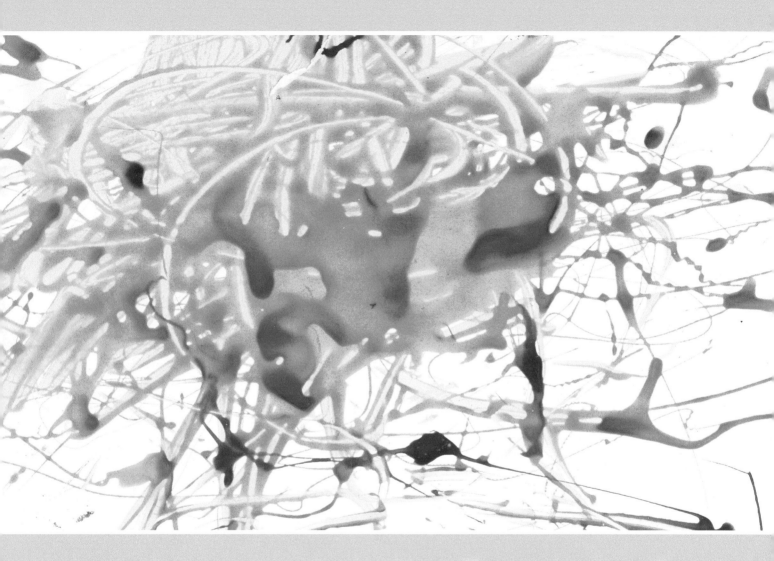

I can tell a grown-up, who
will help me through.

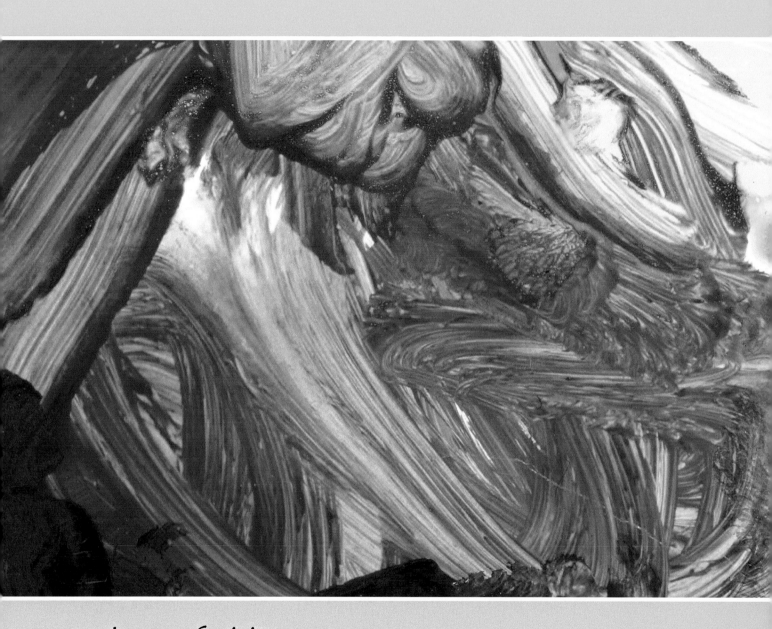

When I feel like crying,
what can I do?

I can always cry if I really
need to.

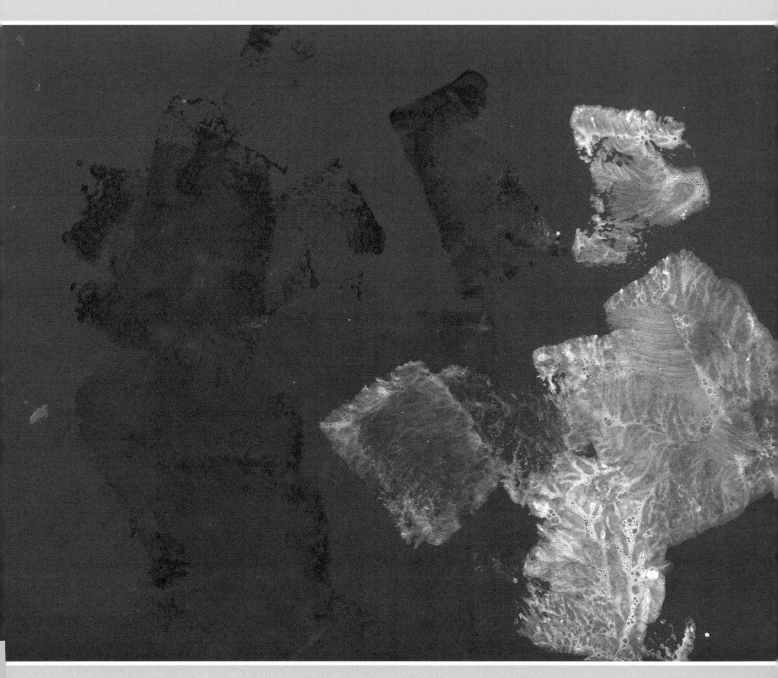

When I feel angry, what
can I do?

I can find someone
to talk to.

These are some things
that I can remember
when I'm feeling low...

I can have quiet time by myself and take it slow. I don't always have to be on the go.

Making friends with someone
new can be something that I
learn with you.

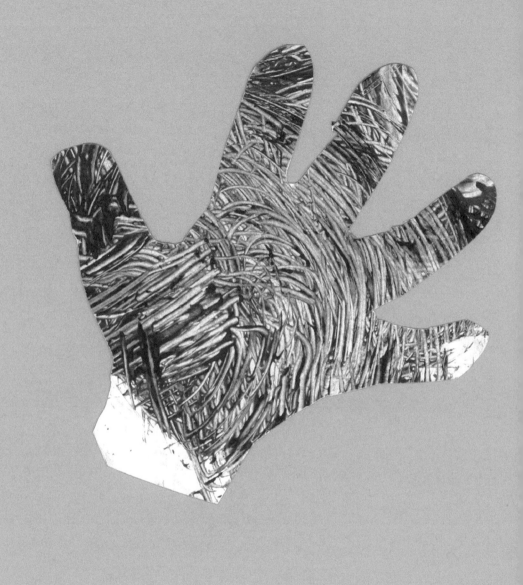

Playing sports in a joyful mood
is something that is great to do.

Thinking of a happy
rhyme makes the sadness
move aside.

I can show others that I care in a special way, which helps me to feel better everyday.

Feeling bored is not very
fun but I can always find
someone.

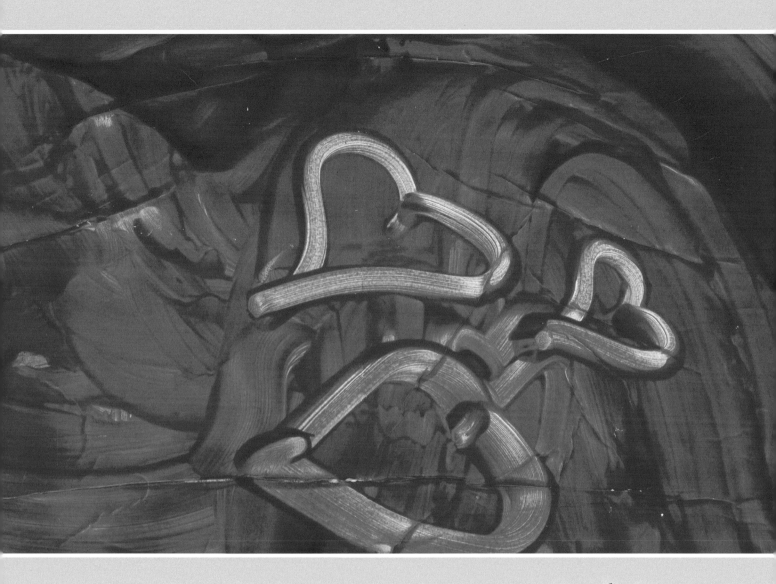

Listening to the feelings
inside, helps to keep me
safe at times.

When I feel _____, I can _____.

When I feel _____, I can _____.

When I feel _____, I can _____.

*Encourage interaction

As a parent, Lola has been learning about internal well-being and emotional development for several years and has found powerful ways of incorporating peaceful practices in her everyday life. Through her journey, she has continued to learn about her inner-self, and this has guided her into acknowledgement of her connection to The Creator through self-expression and artwork.

This creative urge was overwhelming for Lola because she needed to develop a greater understanding of how to positively channel eccentric forms of expression. In challenging times, Lola tuned into her appreciation of unusual forms of eclectic art from around the world and this inspired her to find constructive ways of nurturing her true identity.

Lola worked for many years as a fashion designer where she focused on reinventing the external images of others and after recognising her impact, she decided to reconstruct her own internal image. With a Social Services / Management background, she continues to focus on self-improvement and uplifting the community. Lola's creativity became an inspiration for her son, who at five years of age, became the Co-Author of their first published book.

Her multi-faceted background has given her a lot of life experience, which she uses as teaching tools to support the development of her children's talents. Her desire is to continue working in the community and exploring art with her children, through writing and other creative activities.

Printed in the United States
by Baker & Taylor Publisher Services